TILT

*

Gillian McCain

Hard Press, Inc./The Figures

Cover by Trevor Winkfield, 1996.
Thanks to Larry Fagin, Michael Gizzi, Geoffrey Young and Ed Friedman.
Some of these poems, or earlier versions, have appeared in *Lingo, The World, No Roses Review, Arshile* and *B City.*
Hard Press, P.O. Box 184, West Stockbridge, MA 01266
ISBN: 1-889097-04-7

To the memory of my mother,

Marion "Billie" McCain

Table of Contents

Cloud

It all comes down to a mouth. Don't worry, you won't fall through. It's more like melting. Gels drifting, rhythm of shoulders. Push and it opens. Of course this is only a memory...

Fall

Your world is so beautiful, I made a stopover six years ago and never left. Each day brought a new twist. A clenched fist. A possible future punch. But fear of the marketplace crippled me, living at the acropolis. To continue or turn back. Eventually, a twelve step program. Difficult descent into roughened, impeded language of unthinkable. Nostalgia for intention. My kimono caught on a rising nail...

Silence

In the beginning there was poetry and mystery to the flatness, an offer to fill the earth. What did you do when you got out of bed? The unidentifiable order, caressed into existence cell by cell, took a minute to get used to. A chance to survey the world beyond the moat, at least as far as the beach. Hidden passageways carved from squashed purple light. You walked in the air, waves followed, the moon pulled along on its string. Echo, stone deaf. The staggering lighthouse transformed into a beckoning odalisque. No stuttering feet (after your trip underground). Can you still recognize these sounds? The secret reappeared in the sand. Enter this space, shell.

Skin

To be born in such surroundings was in itself deadly, unvarnished, unsure of what needed to be cut open, but with very good bones. Wrestling with my wherewithal, I knew I missed the mirroring that is so crucial in early childhood. Seeing you through the glass partition signified that the interview would soon begin. I snapped like scissors, suggesting grace, abomination and a temporary relapse from psychoanalysis. I don't know if you know what I'm talking about (which has an upside). I've come to dread these confidential moments, is that so flaky? Cut to: arena [light] [weather] [echo]. The ticket had gouged my face but I was willing to sit still for the event, a stone constituent. The only other continuity in my life has been a self-imposed exile from butter and cream. People (eurotrash) simplify what I say to the point of absurdity. I forget about it then think later did I kill someone? As a problem-solving device, it's in the forefront of my mind all the time. No further comment.

Child

I negotiated my steps carefully to prevent breaking my mother's back. Rebelling to become unstrung, tongue on a frozen monkey bar. The speech therapist tied it behind my back. I was told to trim the forest surrounding my desk. Storytime, a lump in my throat. My upstairs yawn prevented me from using dipthongs. Hedging my bets, my love, the gardener, was not allowed in the dining room. A crack opened up under my shoe. The fact that no one had explained this potboiler had sucked my will to live. Seeds sown long ago were beginning to need power tools. I was, as they say, branching out, requiring a certain amount of "infallible restraint." By that time, I was on drugs, too. No daycare center ever prepared anyone for the immensity of this shit.

Ghost

Tell me about this tic that everyone else seems to find so endearing. Popping up at the right time and place are miscellaneous gestalts that caution us against vice or folly. Did you get lost in the souk? There is a thread running through your fears, false hopes and surrealistic expectations, then left hanging, but ask questions later. My thoughts are my whores, Diderot once said, and we are subject to his spell. Let's start at the start: the oneiric adventures of an insomniac, corner Bleecker & Broadway. Who would believe you, or in you? The NoHo tribes are animist, and not so finicky, but still intolerant of unexamined jugulars. I can empathize with your difficulty editing your world, but as you pierce the balloon, surprises abound inside. You want to be caught looking? Why bide your time until your real life gets underway. Listen, if you didn't get lost in the souk, you never went to the souk. The twitching is your lingua franca, so to speak. But for the moment it is necessary to foreshadow the future by rewinding the present.

Room

I wasn't the most talented but certainly had the most hustle, knew instinctively what the words meant no matter what order. Think of a number. A book is the smallest thing in the world, comes with instructions: to be held for a long time. Too big for one, too small for two, nighttime all day, no residues, no need to haunt anymore. We'll get those to go, know what I'm saying, I'm saying go as far as they'll take you, ambient music is killing me. I don't care how much money it takes, someday we'll catch up to our conjugal breath, I and I. Our minute will beat their hour any day.

Party

(their having been introduced) forgotten minutes later. She moved in mysterious biways. In those days everyday was one of those days. "Three hundred? That's an insult, but because you're an old customer I'll drop her to two." Burst couch, some are breezier than others, she said. Every time a car drove into the service station a bell rang in the bedroom. These humbles are so dreary, like orange ignition smoke on the horizon, smell of burnt glass. They did the locomotion (sliding down the banister). Don't bother bending just push that nut bowl over with your foot. The coat mound contained several negatives, including one of this paragraph. That was a decade of minutes enshrined for their detached involvement. Poetics retouched, thus ruined, we came out all hincty.

Mirror

A hair studied, but I cannot dismiss him as just another fad, e.g. chocolate twigs. Do not touch (unless you plan to buy). The sudden crunch between blinking and sundry figures of speech, no fingerprints. Is he on something new? By the end of the evening, we all found ourselves in the powder room dusting our waxy collarbones, comparing and contrasting. One glance could put any of us over the edge. Breath? A puff.

Interior

You'll like it up here, he says. Time, at least for this moment, feels serene. I lose myself. He's lying on the midnight blue Victorian sofa, head resting on a leopardskin pillow. Ingenuous smile, black humor, red blinds over french doors. As the sun sets the room becomes a chinese after-hours club. It's hard to imagine being unhappy here. I can't stop looking down, with him I will never be anything short of near-sighted. Purple tulips and an orange marzipan fish rest on the gar-goyle table. Viktor Shklovsky said all the good words are faint with exhaustion. I'm still lost. Ginseng-colored hair, translu-cent skin, all your compliments are punch lines, he says. For this rip in time we are partners, our silence is long-winded. The building whistles. How and when did he fall from the sky to my side? In the past, I was a presence that manifested as air. An indescribable ascent toward blind faith. I will miss this.

Journey

Clearly, to understand that there is a way out is of enormous importance. Way out of what? The books with the definitions are obsolete now. His trans-formation from a flower to the flower absent from all bouquets, from the organism to the simulacrum, was consonant with the professor's theory. The talons had to grip something so a wall appeared. With his vitamin B urine and unseen accompaniment he seldom stumbled into deep holes in the dark. That treasure hunt in the stacks was kind of fun, part of the landscape. But putting across the future had its dangers, too. Loudspeaker ears listened in on his projections. The narrative hook was inescapable. When the flood of rumors crested, he had already plagiarized the professor. Far out. The perennial garden shears finally run amok, his hair falling to the earth among the bulbs on the roof he once called home.

Self

Scenic railway dividers. When the content of a whim or impulse fails to be modified by stable aims it becomes primitive and bare, and tends to shift erratically. The lines disconnected or diverged. It would be superfluous to quote any specific examples. Lurking within every tourist is the same point of departure: the nose. Impending impetus. All that had once moved clung tenaciously to the escarpment. No rafters, no roof. I slept in my berth like a hyena. They cut my internals into pie-shaped sequences or souvenirs, a half-hearted experiment which was soon abandoned once we pulled into Biarritz. It was necessary for me to detach in order to become reattached. And what makes you think you're any different? Reciprocating motion, separating us into compartments. Then the tunnel...

Hotel

Overtaken suddenly by a fundamental question. Where does one go to complain? Or suggest. Managing to get a room for the night, I tucked myself in, drownproofing in dreams. The legitimization of vice as pleasure added a further seal to my attachment. To what, I'd like to know. The suggestion box was filled with used kleenex. Sin did not begin in a garden, knocking on miscellaneous doors, pretending not to know who or what was keeping pace with my fate. A huge underdevelopment. I did a good job of hiding my exhibitionism. Why pretend? The unspeakable knocked me out. I ended up on the cutting room floor. No one noticed when the silence learned to speak, prattling on about me like I wasn't even there.

Pool

The man at the bar said, "The mouth of a loose woman is a deep pit." To defy vertigo is to admit that there is nowhere to go but horizontal. My lap crawled in places I didn't even know existed. Aruba, for instance. This added an inauthentic precedent for my already dwindling subconscious. Solution? Kelp injections. My surrogate took on an independent reality. It was useless to pretend any longer, I wasn't Miss Leitmotif, merely girl in bar. The "many dangers" were brushed aside a bit too airily. At bottom, one bubble seemed much like another. I refused to melt away, that's when I blacked out.

Box

Success was achieved only after the viewer realized that she had been deceived. 3D hoogstraatens groped her. Attend to what is within not without. In case of amnesia, always have address on you. Occasionally viewers would jump in but they only wanted an interview. She busied herself tossing plates into heaven. Diagnosis: trompe l'oeil personality disorder. Among her familiars dildoes are contagious. One never knows who is trading. The mirror philosopher said, All answers are given in advance, precluding any questions. Any questions?

History

None of your grope scenes, none of your pleasure scenes, none of your sewer scenes, none of your stale plant regurgitations. Just the moon up there on a pole. Then it's moved [stage left]. Recall all defective memory. Under the rails, the world was fast gone. Poor bog people, skulls flattened in the wind, like us with no props. The most moving story of their silence was their attempt to run down the fading street, blown back by time. Now give the man your money.

Chaos

When we come across a fork in the road, we know there is only one choice. Opticians will tell us otherwise. Now suppose I wanted to make a riddle out of that. Would you pick up on it? That is, would you pick it up? If I told you the answer, rain would leap and the gods would bark. Reactors react. It's all fun and games until someone loses an eye. Stop thief! Hermes personally delivered the package: There are no catastrophes, only perpetual rearrangements. Is this page moving? One small sentence for mankind. None of which affects you as you open the can of beans and eat them with the utensil you found on the highway.

Hair

The wall just went up, and on this occasion it's papered with a rolling-of-the-eyes motif. I'm exasperated, too. I bought stuff I don't need, poems to sew into my lining. Death of Hector, Hotel Wentley, Frost at Midnight. My feelings are killing me, grouchy, but filled with longing. I've got nothing left to scrape. Our government no longer forgives a multitude of sins— I've been ticketed for having been through the loop. This fan makes me appear wind-blown, muted like a heartbeat, but the secret remains in the poems, in the eye of the ringlet. Does that shock you? I'm only telling you what I know, as if you couldn't guess. Nothing to add, too depressed.

Scenery

Not a pretty picture, forest spread-eagled in a cone of light, modulating sound and color through a dark fixation with weather. Only one gate: the eye. A plea for transcendence through blocked steps and glazes. The wall was unscalable, thus ascension meant defecting to phrases embedded in thicket (push and pull of rocks and fiddleheads). Could God handle heavy machinery? No one on the horizon showed any promise of becoming part of the permanent collection. Sun sunk. The resulting fugue state was momentary.

Revolution

It's like this. Plot headquarters is base of operations for the dissection of triangles, but someone has to remain Switzerland. Let it be me. Luke and Marianne are convinced of separation at birth. I'm putting them on hold. Am I an unreliable dramaturge? Luke conceives anti-Marianne, a babe that has never before existed. The real Marianne takes this misreading and runs with it, ushering in her directorial debut. Thus begins the reign of terror. Life is reduced to footnotes on the weather. Luke becomes paralyzed so "storming" anything fails to be an option. He realizes the impossibility of interpreting beyond her words the simplest feelings shown in Marianne's face, sneering or smiling. Mild precipitation casts doubt on her heart. The muse could always rally the masses, but being at a loss for words is such a thankless job. Why couldn't they just settle for the same fantasy? There is no way to explain it (at least in this language). But for all the hubris, not to mention creepy insularity, I envy them their carelessness. Is ignorance the seed of their torment? Nah. The longest line between two points is the least detected. The receiver dangles, still moist.

War

I'll tell you a funny story. They wanted to stay close to the center of things, out of their element, to be sure, but that was in large part why they had come. Both enjoyed a controlled amount of fear, low rumble drowned out by their own pulses. FIREBALL. They begged the chambermaid to hide them in the dryer. Few reminders of sky above, sinkhole below. At last, a predicament that had nothing to do with "channeling emotional power." They tried to straddle their two different fjords, but just kept tumbling, moving deeper and deeper apart. Her pedal pushers ripped during the inspection tour of the munitions dump. The silence of self-storage cost them a bundle.

Holes

There are many murders there, they call it Gulf. Japanese businessmen examine the openings scientifically. Smells like it's been a long time. Allowed their dreams, they guard against inappropriate feelings like anger or mental molar extraction. They may touch not just look. However, to show respect, take care to leave a little to the imagination, like a cum sandwich. Or a restraining order on the sun. Rinse and spit. Belated attempts to master earlier trauma, gently down the stream.

Magic

The note said: You will attend a gathering where certain rituals will be performed. Bubbles could be seen rising from the bottom of the beaker. In the next room, the haircut began. "How would you feel about us taking it up a little higher this time?" Blink. And what? Make me look like a retard? Heavier and heavier. The itinerary was as follows: 1) Extract coin from ear canal, 2) Speak in run-on-sentences to save time, 3) Figure out how long I had to last. Groggy to the point of tedium, determined to be reconstituted as a view with a point, I avoided drugwar crossfire by hiding behind Bubbles. The fourth wall was my frame of reference, cascading down the runway. Is that perhaps why I have so few lines? I knew I had to find something liquid to believe in, and dis-appearances seemed as logical as anything else. This was one retard who wouldn't reappear as a fistful of pigeons.

Separation

People. I knew some of them, but not now. On the moon, I wander among the many pot holes. Their shadows make me feel planet-stricken. Display model #1: clusters of magnetic liquids. I would like to uncover the mystery of the scrim. Will I rise to the occasion when it decides to fall by? A tiny walled-off angel lays an egg. A secret life—the ruminations of a creature that walks without legs, eats without a mouth, breathes without lungs, feels without nerves, then divides and conquers. What happens when you try to squeeze a puddle of gravity in your hand? It dissolves into hundreds of silver eggs. Me too. The incubation period was over. Display model #2: people backed up into a dark corner. Unearthed puzzle, same the moon all over. Next stage? Parachute, the final explanation arising as I make my slow descent.

Orange

The tulip fell flat on its face, the sky curled around whatever was available over Florenceville. Finger cymbals dinging, or a marbled tongue. No need to feel plugged in or extended. The current fantasy is berserk, which is not to say other adjectives fail as they hunch over the hole. Are they beeped, the discovery of yet another point of entry? We civilians fear sleep without a crush, the seeds of our flashes are dried on the radiator then eaten as snacks. Forked perspectives of dark eyebrows. After pureeing, contents can be combed through hair and left on indefinitely. She arrived at the door holding a pumpkin with the baby's limbs protruding out of carved holes. Gauze around the hands and feet rounded out the effect. The river crept up to the road, swam across it. Butch opened the cooler, took out a Moosehead, and propped up the tulip. He gazed at the zamboni circling the rink, brushing off the blade fuzz. If mixed with berries, leftovers can be used as blush.

Road

Let's go watch the ice break up. You don't like it, split. The only problem with the pick-up was her dependence on the man with the snow plow. She said no hands when he touched her. She was stooped by sentence formation, bent on hanging out in departure lounges. The county was so small, it seemed ridiculous that she couldn't spit it out. What had once been fluid was now jagged. Daredevilism used to mean snowmobiling across the river, now it's sleeping under scratchy sheets in Best Westerns with no chainlock. The digital revolution made no impression, she still believed that (sex) success was based on meritocracy. The story that interested her most was one that was potentially her own. Strike that. The story that interested her most was one that she potentially owned.

Trees

Zeke in slow motion. Winds of change had fallen upon him, he didn't dig it one bit. I witnessed his Reichian vocal chord exercises, romantic blackouts, counter-transferences. Diagnosis: damsel in distress syndrome. Locust lockjaw carrying on an obsessive monologue, mostly about himself. I half-listened, flipping the leaves to a new scene, a nouveau former self, fresh moral blandishments, a different pretty face on each arm. Dripping. He was frisked, busted and cuffed, facedown on the macadam. What does will look like? Not pink, violent.

Family

The memory was there, but every time his mind came near it, gypsies appeared on the piazza selling plastic ears to commemorate the event. Love existed in the presence of a blanched wrong at the right time. But let me tell you about his people, a five layer cake representing some sort of continuity for those who require it. His colorblind sister created fortresses out of roquefort, while he dug his own little moat in the sugar. Pet peeve: peasants. His mom insisted his robes match the outdoor carpeting. Subliminal makeover: his fingerprints were manhandled in an attempt to make the permanent look temporary. Communicating by proxy became a bourgeois hang-up, i.e. a daily occurrence. He was out to break up the narrative, change the p.o.v. Could any of these scenes be cut without disrupting the entire old boy network? Later, strapped to a life support mouth, he decided that trauma always led him gently toward an independent dystopia. Anyway, it beat Anna Karenina.

Thought

We will not act civilized in this fucking city. Loneliness and boredom came upon us quietly and unexpectedly, usually after all the basic needs had been provided for. The distinct society tore at everything in reach, including us, caught helplessly inside. I was living in a studio above a chinese take-out on the Main. The moon was in the house of dreams on the eve of the lengthy putdown. We moved through the time zones, reappearing as pirates or frequent flyers. He referred to psychology as a "nasty little subject" that excludes everything we would want to know. No chintz in his living room nor bowls of waxed fruit. He offered a shoulder to cringe on, but the photos he showed us aged me ten years. Thank you sir I'll modify my behavior. What we should have asked him was, When you walk down the Main, do the waters part? We fought our way through the separatists, born to observe, not die.

Direction

In a forest of bending and swaying forms, a girl could not find her way. She camped out on a jagged bluff. She preferred to live in her own little words, but people were everywhere. She had sympathy for the camera that panned aimlessly in the bushes. Finally alone, she bedded down on a knoll of pine cones and dreamed about the goat boy. She wrapped her bag around him and they entered the zone together. He gave her a present: this cone. They ate berries and caught bees in mason jars. For days they lived quietly, counting backwards. Then he said, It's time for some new faces. She refused to move when he tried to squeeze by. Then she was awake. There was plenty of elbowroom left in her universe, her words. Yet somehow she knew that she wasn't the only lost girl who believed in ending up where you began.

Memory

More desire came along to take its place (don't blink). She stepped off the plane complete with instructions. She was neighborhood. I was at the age where hitting someone meant you liked them. Don't lock yourself in the closet, the alligator will swim beside you to the island where you will begin your program. When strategically ripped, her mind ceased being a little supper club. All the great passions based on distance; they promise us that future cities will be adorned with monuments dedicated to her; her head and nose an upside-down mortar and pestle, her beard an obelisk. Still more to come.

Nothing

Some puppets never learn that mirror images are illusions, bumping up against themselves. In a locked room, sleep was one bitter put-on (no sound from the tree falling at the foot of the bed). Trudging through the lake emergency area was an invitation to a lazy fall into the ditch of mixtured string. One numb arm points a finger at the long cold stare from the sky, face to face with bandaged rain. The lightning bolt ceases to remember itself. A real boy begins his lesson on joint maintenance. Not happy, blessed. A man is a small thing and the night is very large and full of wonders.

Touch

I'm a girl, there aren't many of us left. Time to take the bullet by the hole. Certain designs rely on not being seen. I never denied I was just an assemblage of staves. Collapsing around us. This means not taking our rooms so seriously. We can't see the wallpaper (pink scotties) or a misprint in the proof. Sometimes skin has to do all the talking. Recto, verso. But can you even enter them, speeding through the story? Once upon a time a golf tee punctured our waterbed. I thought I was going to live forever, immoral. I thought a lot of things, the court artist had trouble with my nose. Elongated, normal. A little lower.

Friday

I can't come. It's these antidepressants. I'm getting smaller. Now what? Take my band-aid off? No way. Sea shells occasionally bite, you can't not agree with that. But I didn't have any designs on his feet, honest. Now I gotta do his tail, stop him from flying off the spatula. Remember when I was just a little tiny rubber stamp? I went around notarizing every dick on the block to get to level two. Blank mind goulash. Now at level seven there's a few more plebes I wanna morph. I've opened my own scenario shop. It's a pleasant locale for egging people on. No scallops today. I'm game for any injunction that tom or harry serves me, a date, say, with a peripatetic bicycle messenger or a disillusioned paralegal. Once I reach my peak I'll evaporate gracefully. No one will have an inkling of where I went.

Laboratory

Not to mention the fact that the extremely sloppy copy job undermined the whole purpose of reproduction, a morbid act involving my entire personality. The lines were bleeding all over the floor, signaling from elsewhere. But could elsewhere be copied? This ceremony served a specific function: to stun or intoxicate white men in an environment as sterile as possible. A totally new interpretation of original sin, the result of some massive coup d'etat. See my exegesis of The Tree of Knowledge in the History of Tribeca, Vol. 11. A deliberate slap in the whiskers to the Board of Directors. What are you? Mice not men.

House

We are beginning to feel cramped as the tide drags the sea away. The innovation of reducing the hour to a Delphic seven or eight minutes has yet to be adopted. A teaspoon of sugar in the water helps the lilacs live longer. Your wife's success has increasingly made her disciples feel free to slip out from behind her aegis, letting the world learn the simple facts about their real roles. No more dinner guests. We sit by the electric oven, feet propped up on the open door. The turret is blurry through the dirty windows, the sky the color of sea-weed. Your room is no longer suitable for someone your age. It's high time you grew out of bulletin boards. I knock and enter and ask about the time change. Misfired synapses result over my unexplained shore leave. The radio is suddenly abducted as high tide is tacked onto our timers. On the beach, the children dip themselves then roll in the sand. They come up solid. Based on a novel.

Light

Clockwise from top: nervousness at revealing herself, armchair fascism, a blindness to gut reactions. Emptied in an instant, her face passed the point of no deposit. You know exactly what I mean. They traipsed through the city in drowsy battalions. Rabbit ears emerged from the shadows, useless, but unavoidable. Dusk collapsed as her pupils dilated. She moved through the fair, fascinated by the evanescent possibility of eternity appearing in the guise of a one-night stand at the Center for Attention. At least that's the way my memory has colored it. Is the mike on? The focal point of her analysis was to reclaim her projections and come to grips with the fact that they were deeply superficial. All she had ever wanted was a little privacy to continue her socratic dialogue with the screen.

Life

Solitude is the perpetual and daily horror of the prisoner, whose final piece of confinement is the elf. Go to your cubby-hole. Refusing to trust the invisible hand, my palm imbedded in the vagabond concrete of Grauman's Chinese. I imagined a sphere of light engulfing me like mummy wrappings (for maximum protection). Hooked on you-know-what, the only organism that touched my body was the occasional incubus. Is hysteria any less intoxicating when it is this neatly choreographed? This is not a roman a clef designed for your private delectation. What is the color of the sky in your world? Don't answer that.

Tilt

The big, big try of the jet getting off the ground. All too soon those mean vocal shakes; too far the original itinerary; soon confusing signals at astonishing speeds, destination moon. The ear focused on the smooth and brutal "I" emptying out, and the thousand fine lines cloaking the obvious: one line only, ten items or less, one mind split over the pros and cons, nine reasons supporting the dignity of exile. Climbing over the city, swinging out above the sea, fragmented only when interrupted by thought.

Dream

The result is instinctual atrophy and hence disorientation in everyday situations. Mom called up the stairs, There's a boy from the musical Tommy at the door. A vocalist who doesn't trust the genre. The unexpected pursued obliquely, harder to get a grip on than mercury balls. Did you sense the emptiness? Tooth hanging on by a weak thread. Does my voice sound like yours at last? Aural caramel? The saga continues: a flying koan smashes the storm windows. There is only one current running through all this confusing circuitry. Not. I pour myself a glass of lobster champagne. I spot Iceland on the map. Enucleating it without scissors, I suffer deeply over this cold, lonely crime.

Sex

Come here often begins at home. At least we're through with our own lives now (hitting nails on heads). We manipulated the truth together (peer alignment during rubbernecking). The bar was named The Library so nobody could accuse us of lying. When it spun we were the only patrons moderately proportioned, and that was the first time I used fuck as an adjective. They put detergent in the fountain, the ones that play that song "Burn Down the Mall." Plus covers for fans with feathered bangs. Try to improve your vocabulary and those types will avoid you like any other textured surface. Lemme tell you about my cousin Buzz, who attracted petals like essential irons. Good trope, dude. But there are no slots for others, and thus discomfort in not knowing how to categorize (harp solo). The wraparound skirt shimmered when it walked over the grate. Next please never went over easy. Don't say we didn't warn you, fuckface.

Travel

We refused to rely on historical themes that couldn't be trusted, e.g. manifest destiny, good neighbor policy, great society, hemlock. We couldn't just lean back and let it all unspool. Sybarites on a pilgrimage, we had a peer group of billions. How they discovered our whereabouts is still a mystery. We raped and pillaged our way through a lifetime of non-encounters. Trekking up and down antique shortcuts, we slept in tool sheds, acquired blurry phone numbers on cocktail napkins, and developed a fierce case of Tourette's. Dissolve to a drumlin: icy. We pondered our nightly quandry of where to eat. In Hamburg we got so wrecked we forgot to piss on the other band's amplifiers. The scenery was huge, constricting, unconscionable. We plagiarized it immediately, regenerating consciousness into swallow-like bites. Contemplating these marvels only further reminded us that we had never left East Orange. The summit talk proved to be nothing more than a sleep-over.

Blind

I'm drunk. Unfortunately, the political context of this date encourages such a turning inward, especially among the shortsighted, because there is nothing attractive about the situation at the federal level. If they didn't want me to come they shouldn't have invented me. I mystify them in the way they like to be mystified, my community hours can wait a few days. Turn it up, the dial's on the right. These flapping wings in my eardrums preclude access to miscellaneous information without a suction cup. I don't want to turn this confession into a nolo contendere, let's not and say we did. Another dreamy season, this time you may turn out to be winter. It's the others who come and go, not merely shortsighted but crosseyed, straightlaced, deaf.

Truth

At the marathon poetry symposium Mr. Baraka was merciless in his critique of Miss Myles' lack of politesse. Milk was souring in the rectory. Mr. Mac Low quoted the late Mr. Cage: Now I am saying it. Ms. Harryman stated, I had no imagination, growing up. The marxist poet spilled seltzer on the floor and ordered me to clean it up. It's hard to get good help these days. Next time you go shopping, notice what reverie you are in, Ms. Neilson said. Ms. Wasserman and I observed from the sidelines. Let's open the '88 now, she suggested. People began establishing camps—blue collar vs. white collar vs. Peter Pan. Most people's utopias sound unbearable, I whispered to Ms. Wasserman. It all comes down to just getting laid, she replied. Down, down, down. How do you like us now? We enjoy a cheap laugh at your expense as much as the next Ms. (Dancing is simply out of the question.) Ms. Barg played rap music with offensive lyrics on the high-low panel. Mr. Savage approached me and declared, We seem to be having a security problem. With that, Ms. Wasserman passed me the flask. Mr. Sanders described hideous psychological techniques that can turn an orderly citizen into a foaming maniac. Bi-polar audience members asked too many already-answered questions. The high before the crash, Mr. Rothschild commented. Reactionaries descended upon revolutionaries just as Mr. Andrews called his fellow panelists "self-huggers." The banging ideologies oppressed me. In the colonies, peace is concluded after each side has been given ceremonial freedom to strike the other. Safe on top of the piano, Mr. DiCaprio studied us for his upcoming role. I'll wait for the paperback, Ms. Wasserman screamed up at him. The following week, Mrs. Hornick presented the counter-revolution. The President is making me pay more taxes. He is a coarse, lower middle class man. Seconds later, Sexton Fragosa tip-toed into the parish hall and handed me a note: No future in pork rinds. After the wrap-up panel, the collars meekly disassembled. The milk had finally turned to cheese.

Game

I'm happy to turn the patient over to you, personally. During the freezing moment on the landing I noticed a tear in the screen. They have a right to as much blood as they need. This leads to a peaceful ending, but there is nothing to wash it down with. It's a mistake to think of an act as a justification of being, bent over double. Had the orgone box been tampered with? Could the neighbourhood children be right? My sticky daydreams have become tiresome. I get a feeling that I'm being reborn in loam, unable to do calisthenics. By the way, I've given her something to help her sleep, a high speed chaser. Let's try to leave a few signs lying around for the incoming players.

Walls

The house was on the outskirts of the city, I guess I mentioned that before. Boldly pulling the curtains aside, I stared at the serfs, stunning in bunches but individually hideous. After lunch I busied myself by dividing thoughts and expressions into separate categories. A harmless interlocuter obstructed the view, and a crucial passage in Strunk & White was obscured. Naturally, I spoke of this matter to my comrade, who to my great astonishment reacted with derision and anxious defensiveness. I felt obliged to remind him that we were codependents in neutralizing the abhorrent. Such joint ventures were often subject to scrutiny by upstanding members of the community. My role as suzerain didn't stop them from forcing me down on all fours, chained to my hapless divine right. Whose side are you on? The partition would crumble under the weight of experience. Insidious and inflexible, all that was left us was theoretical violence. But I was moved (sometimes).

Lines

The human heart is an extraordinary organ. Pump pump. The moog melodies wafted upwards. Mooing. Where does blue stop and nothing start? The trapeze along the 49th parallel. Come here often? The sidewalk mails its engraved invitations. RSVP: strung out. Have you ever felt a gentle fall? Dumbfounded angels suffering from uncertain vertigo. Blind to the cracks. The milkman comes and takes away the baby. It's hard to say goodbye this way. The question is not whether it's true, but why is it so important now? You understand the difference, don't you? Anyway, it was all in the papers.

Freedom

Edwidge didn't meet the requirements to become a dictator so she slapped on a new phase and exploded the illusion that girls can't piss over balconies. She was jaded, unlisted, and had a dowry of nine cows. An intrepid vagabond moving within window displays, she knew that feet were amongst the hardest organs to fake. Absence of motivation made her implicitly tolerated. It isn't suprising that she left everything unfinished, eternally drooping, and plunged into the land beneath as her wooden shoes floated to the top. The hang of it was firmly within reach (between the sun and the earth). Suddenly, without gravity, she welcomed heights, depths and distances. Gushing from a hidden source, the epiphany was so obvious that it mocked her: empty the metaphors and the peripheries cave in. This was the final hoop but did she jump? No, her bloodlines enforced a blockade. She became the power that dribbled and eventually was sent home with a note.

Letter

Just writing to see if anything happened this month, if anything. So many people told me to say hello: Madge, who broke up with Midge, and Harold Bloom said to keep the electric scissors, he's got plenty. True, I've become a conversation piece, but look who's talking. Give me mud and I will paint that pistachio skin of yours. Last spring the army worms were so bad that the southeast side of the cottage became invisible, and the last straw, Teenie said, was when I vacuumed the lawn. Once she moved back to our one-product town, her life went right on blossoming. Here in the outback it's so quiet you can hear a ching! Gulls skim the Bay of Fundy, clamdiggers look like weeble-wobbles in galoshes. So you like working at the video store, that's good. Teenie says I have split-level-ambition-disorder. I heard a local comment, "She always makes perfect sense after she's been drinking." But I say there's nothing wrong with my throttle. Lying in the hammock, I occasionally review alternative courses of action I might have taken. Who really knows anything about franchising? Perhaps I'll take a stab at it. You say you did some research on the subject (message received). The problem is, I like to begin things with no preconceived notions. Anyone can handle trauma, but only the truly brave can endure suspense. My challenge is to somehow animate this hallowed environment, and I intend to succeed where others have flunked. I understand your inability to comprehend my mission, but I do recall during your weekend stay your request to quote get me outta here unquote. Not many people can say they took permanent root on the island where Roosevelt summered. But what had once been a retreat has become an evacuation. Uh oh, Ward's calling me to come back in and squirt those damn fruitflies. Keep me posted about poor Mary Eagle Dog's candida.

Hospital

You've all heard the shark stories. The mantle of adulthood was shed, thus ensued the early flush of revolution. Spansules of nostalgia induced a compulsive desire to publish what wasn't happening. Miracle #1: The resident hairdresser found honey-coated almonds lodged in her scalp. She knew what was eating her up so she coerced the tribes of enduring strains to do their rounds backwards. A bored voice became the harbinger of her P.O.W. status. She cast all predictions and forecasts aside, knowing that her job was to entertain and instruct. Always swimming, never sleeping. Cranky angels controlled the metaphors: tenses, cycles, spaces. Miracle #2: For once there was enough time to contemplate the mysterious circumstance of the holy boomerang. What exactly did you want her to confess? After crossing the border into anomaly territory, the snapdragons arrived C.O.D. Time would not demand more intense cutting. Miracle #3: She finally received tenure.

Newspaper

He had a voice that whispered like tires. He drove with one hand, the other gripped her jutting hipbone. They chauffeured three parties in monochromatic blazers to the Waldorf, dropped them off at the side door. The one in burnt sienna said, "Honey, we didn't come here to peel carrots." She laid her head in his lap and stared up at the columns. Steam billowed. They were unable to examine, comprehend, or guide their own thought processes, emotions, and ensuing behavior. When he tried to reflect on himself, objects appeared closer than they really were. Vertebrae poked through the paragraphs, an edifice complex. "Upscale intimacy" was a number he tried on her from time to time, knowing that it failed utterly to mask his past digressions and future cataclysms. The goosebumps, she soon learned, were in the details, this, that, and the other. It had been ineffectual to turn a blind eye on their trust fund bohemianism by inventing a fable based on blue collar roots. Nothing, essentially, had happened. How far down the pike of their inertia has this short journey taken us? Not very. The option is up for grabs. Even though this is their story, the public has a right to know.

Night

In a few minutes all hell would break loose. Or at least some of it. Surfaces and depths were brought into focus by the return of silence. Her lazy eye was frozen on Magnetic Hill. Men Working. Then the curve came out of nowhere. From that day on she drove at parade-speed, paranoid that there were no guard rails between her and Dead Water River. A pit stop at the bootleggers was a radical departure from her usual non-recusant nature. She didn't arrive unimpaired but no one noticed (the hootenany was already well under way). (Pushkin) the burnt orange cat on the sofa, the one reaching for the clamato juice. She refused to smooth Owl's ruffled feathers when he expressed concern that she might be an "outsider." But Pussy stuck up for her. Would she recognize either of them in a line-up? She stuffed herself with orchids and left just as The Cicadas counted off 96 Tears. Swerving around roadkill, she reassured herself that she was like a rock, spitting out the last word with smug immodesty. But the classic you'll be sorry refrain eroded all resolve. Mica burned in her palm as she reached for warm milk ...

Sun

Magazine Girl made a fence with her arm around the loose-leaf. Lots of onomatopoeia, dig? Girls go by sounds, boys by pictures. The objects do the breathing. Unfortunately, nerve endings never end. The lipstick dropped from the ceiling into her pocket, a product of phantom limb pain. Jacob knew that according to the survey he was a certified pressed flower. If he hated anything it was the fluctuating weight of "issues." Even when the lighting was perfect he felt inclined to comment, "there's not much to work with here." In his mind there was just enough space for a pool table (and a pressing obsessive compulsive disorder). If they're too tight, his theory was, just lie down to zip them up. As a wrestler he grappled with the problem of measured servings. Magazine Girl heard a sound in the basement so she checked the attic (guess which one never leaves the apartment). One leap year there just wasn't enough chloropyll to keep either of them alive.

Mind

So I'm a chronological primitivist, what of it? Today, I took a walk in the light-manufacturing district, where everything's been converted. It's a strange coincidence that we both ended up here as converts (or perverts), you to the Parti Quebecois, me to escapism. Unthinkable, isn't it! All that was needed was clarity (or entropy) in some chamber of my inner ear. Surrendering to the social pressures of the day, I became a strong silent tape with an air of solitary confinement. Terrorist whispers on heavy rotation obliterated a petit mort's poignant denouement. When deja vu's differ, whose, ultimately, should take precedence? History is doomed to refund itself all over again, I ponder as I sit knitting at the foot of the guillotine.

Shadow

Didn't have the heart to wake you, that's why. They wanted to send students who could please the king, to handle him. His lands weren't exactly sprawling. We started with materials that explode after being cooled down, the invisible drip that destroys the mind. We divided into groups and my share was the usual invocation to Jerry for a jerry-built universe. It all came true, thus constituting the most profound sense of anarchy, or irony, e.g. matching shoes and socks, a toppled throne. Under the sun I learned what it means to be a minion, now I won't settle for anything less. Seeing your face on-screen triggered a flood of feelings, read em to you later.

Circle

It took too long to inculcate the importance of clock-like precision to protect oneself from change or novelty. Spotlight on cocktails. Drifting off, I have my recurring dream: paralyzed by my own fundamental sweetness of being, unable to apply sunscreen. By the way, have you ever experienced impotence? It's vicious. Look behind you to your five o'clock, see if there's a shadow. Train your headlights on the sunflower-man, the brother with the bushy beard, his face in crowned ecstacy as he remembers the day's misinformation. Memory is the wave of the future. The goal lies ahead of us. No, make that behind us.

Rock

We have come here within this roofed cave, boiled by the storm. Outside, the blockhouse has been torched by a local arsonist, tongued by shadows. Through ripped holes other holes appear. The neighborhood girls burrow into blankets, solid footing undulates in their wake. Hereinafter roads dissolve in albumen, and we bring up a delicate topic — the thatch has been pried open. Time rises to a stop, drooling. Not to wish this on anyone: to have shut the thick cloud and locked the gate.

Other

Please allow me to introduce myself. Lightning took the night off, its counterpart crackled quietly. Not a pathetic fallacy. I'm already one warm body. Housework has become my raison d'etre, always have something depressing to do. Nonetheless, I reserve the right to go off in a different direction. Divine intervention. But do not allow yourselves to be jumpstarted so easily. The authorities are wrong, there is life in a vacuum. I have asked repeatedly to be able to play by myself. Act I, Scene I: I leave the Burger King, missing the other that suddenly melted off my side.

Time

What ever happened to carpe diem? No bones about it: my goal was oblivion. I was reared on simple storytelling, franchised legends that created puppets of patented blarney. I only became a black sheep after a disagreement over succession, you fill in the gaps. The speckled belly of rapid breaths has spawned a convenient amnesia, from riches to rags to a gag order, but it was better than what happened to Michael Milken. Last call? Don't mind if I do, still not feelin those feelins, like a patient etherized upon a waterbug. Funny faces, remembrance of their names is guaranteed if the stockholders will sing their songs. The one on top is me, arm around old blue eyes, snapped back when it really meant something. Then the red carpet stopped rolling out. To this day I swear that I was indeed pushed. Presently, my plan is to camp out here round-the-clock and then, imperceptibly, inch-by-inch my way toward the credit lines, before they, and I, roll off the edge into what I was looking for in the first place.

Death

The field is filled with children dressed as fairies. They suffer the eclipse gladly, pinned down in flight, drenched in their petals. Nightcaps on the landscape, a wash of strolls. The spirits are peeled in one motion, like shrimp, converted to shrunk footprints, flapping. Negatives hung out to dry. Then it pours, a strange poured timbre, the world breaking in, lumbering through the arcades. The forest dwindles to a spongy cluster, creating a stranglehold on light. Potato blossoms bend in the gust. The sky returns and the clearing suddenly becomes silent.

Cat

I have been chosen to take this message back to the world, and I don't work with just any city. I'm fixated on the placement of objects, and whiplash helps to focus my attention: swoosh, hand sliced over head. I fall in love with them when they're teenagers and date them once they're middle-aged. Immediately they prop the ladder up against the column, which I discovered is the raised eye entry into their often haphazard techniques. Hairball. I'll feel better once I throw it up. I'm regaining the ability to maintain my dignity under adverse conditions, lost in the twirling thread of enamel. There is no garden path. In my own graceful way I'm merely continuing my search for the perfect room, preferably one with a windowseat, looking out to sea.

Car

Even when confused by wires, ponder which sets of knees fit into the grand scheme (before the wheel). A curtain blows something along these lines. The letter grows up to be everybody. Adam. Basic training consisted of you-ought-to-get-outside-more-often. Don't ever say I tried to tell you. There is no counter-irritant after the intitial explosion, or first bite. Never allow anything more tenderness than God does. Been there, seen it, did it, admittedly over-medicated (like a low impact flashback). So sad for so long, now numb with occasional mild highs. Careful of the swallows when you open the garage door.

Gap

My best thinking always occurs during these gaps. The room had been designed with my arrival in mind. If you collect enough corners you can get rid of the snakes. Occasionally I have dreams where I'm nurtured, but a big part of me (my Slovakia) simply doesn't care. Every time I hear myself apologizing, I snap the elastic, worn like a bracelet. Then my shadow temporarily disappears, leaving its stretch marks all over the walls. Fading red coils. In my next life, tiptoe. Although I feel dependent on my three minute share, I still don't care for the look of this crowd, and it's not like my bodyguard gives a shit. An open door policy allows for a wide variety of urchins. Sore thumbs. Tonight, my fantasy is buzzing above and below but I can't feel it inside. Gotta reach down in there and pull out the stopper. Uh oh, projectile creative visualization motion sickness. The riffraff can clean it up at their leisure.

You

I'm a hair consultant, color and what not. I want to make a million dollars. I do daily visualizations of an undiscovered hue, a new you. It all passes by in a blur. Once I get the patent, all that remains is board approval. In the meantime, I'm leasing a painting: The Triumph of Marius — wild horses, tambourines and what not. Let's face it, I'm always trying to escape. I thumb through back issues, promise of a better life, common as dirt. My former boyfriend (whose street name means he's the one with the inflammation) says I have to admit I need help. All I know is that I want this stage of my development to be over. I can't change my stratum, no matter how long I keep scrubbing and scrubbing. What's with that fucking board? What would you do if you were I? But you're you, aren't you, the old you, without the pink streaks. Look, I never claimed the solution was water-resistant. What I lack in credibility I make up for in sanguinity. And I have the stains to prove it.

Bond

Doone is up and coming (so everyone keeps reminding me). This is not the box to search for the forces that condition motivation in each instance; for motivation varies, being always proportional to the ease of viewpoint analysis and the obviousness of the meaning of the anxiety present. If I want to buzz her in, I'll buzz her in. [Brief racket caused by luggage wheels on hardwood floor]. Air kiss. Here she is, smashing in her lilac skirt with little footstools on it, a light breeze from the slammed door blowing her bangs northwest, but I can see it's taking all her strength to get straight. We know that criticism is essential to creative thinking, so I'm going to level with her: I can see her through the box. I say, Young lady, don't expect me to cut the cord, repetitive strain injury or no. She's running away, okay? Going to say she's gone, walking to say she went. Her jumpy knee, part of the collective unconscious. Nothing is cut out for her (except the words). The next message will be more positive, more upbeat.

Park

While I look at Leg Show, Grace reads W. She points out the face of a friend superimposed on a leather clutch. The necks of the old guard continue to stretch. They spy and scribble. We're not glued to this bench, even though our afternoons have lost their meaning. Grace says she prefers me all slouched down like a bored kid. She tells me I'm a reflector, not an initiator. Someone we don't know stops and says, Gum? Grace refuses to look up. Go float, she says. Don't mind her, it's just that she's had it up to here with our first lady's aborted promises, and the municipal government's recent statement that the bleeding is not caused by rocks. Grace and I look at it this way: the sky will never reach us, affirmative action or no. When it rains, we take it personally. Someone standing on a box inspires us to split the scene. As we make our way toward the gate, volunteers whisper sense, sense, sense. We don't have that kind of money, replies Grace.

Factory

At night, the brides scoot, gut reacting to bad directions. Although their tonsils were taken out long ago, the desire for tonsilitis remains. In the dead of winter they flit around the quad like moths. It's the same old story, handed down by flowers barking at the moon, though the traps and snares never reach a thematic conclusion. Tonight, dear butler, don't forget to take the lid off, as some girls have so many planets inside them they require extra leg room, and the carbohydrate loading often induces a sporadic kicking motion from the mezzanine. The beauty of these girls is that as long as they're stored in darkness for the first three weeks, they're destined to grow to mammoth proportions, and can look forward to a daily allowance of double-jointed bliss in their next incarnation. Just then I woke up, broke, tired, hungry, horny.

Love

This is my friend. I call him Egg. He always seizes the moment for a few seconds more than is good for him. He's a beautiful cat. A large popcorn is the only thing that ever comes between us. Egg is selling his title because it's too much responsibility, plus he hates the Fatherland. I'm under Egg's thumb and I like it a lot, it's warm down here. But now I have to go to work. My commission is one cent per flyer. Egg says I'm devious, and where there is corruption there is also desire for a better life. I'm in constant motion against the current in order to maintain my spot. And now, Egg would like to say a few words. Thanks, Gillian. I'm seizing this moment in memory of the late Howard Cossell, who commented on "the moral flabbiness born of the exclusive worship of the bitch-goddess SUCCESS." My earldom is spiritually bankrupt, just like Jack Kerouac's raincoat, but I'd like to remind everyone that I plan on paying back every piaster.

Scene

It was a dark and stormy night. Doone contemplated Western thought as the saloon doors swung open. "Watch where you aim that bottle," the hero said to no one in particular. Doone loved men who looked like they'd always get her home in one piece, but never asked where she was at. Bang bang bang bang. So, she concluded, those who are grasping with regard to these things — wealth, honors and bodily pleasures — gratify their appetites and in general their feelings and the irrational element of the soul. Spin that bottle. The thing you have to understand is that Doone is not in a good head space. All her reactions are dictated by a time release capsule, and once those little guys get going they don't have all day. Down the hatch, Doone, take it like a man. Let's see how you handle the situation this time — without a gun.

Gift

You'd better sit down for this. Some families put an angel on top, others a star; still others a raspberry omelette; it depends on what's handed down. I have just the thing at home for picking that up. The verbs are often doubtful, but the nouns contain actions, each one proof of an incident where feeling and expression contradict each other. I'm not sure how high off the ground I am. It's exhilarating the way life catches hold wherever it can find shelf space. Slice my brain horizontally, discover America. Don't bother wrapping it. The grand narrative of progress has nothing to do with saving time.

Dive

Pink dress, pink shoes, pink attitude. She took me to a restaurant where they had pictures of poodles on the menu, in a neighborhood where I had degraded myself in the past. Just once, she said, I'd like to be able to read your face. Me, I always skip the descriptive parts, jump straight to the dialogue, hop past the area where the people squat. She said, You don't even know I exist. She was right. It was too late to become invisible, but I knew instinctively that the bends could be prevented by ascending slowly, in stages. I broke the surface, gasping, but by the time I got home my courage was lost — I'd been too long risking my life to lung infections and collection agents. The traditional glass cannon was blown up. I was cited for contempt for referring to the judge as "the presiding muppet." What's a pink attitude anyway? Whatever.

City

The haze was actually purple. I stared down at the elevated freeway, the folks diminished by psycho-socio dwarfism. Frederick came home and mixed me a drink. We had only recently melded, after he leapt fully formed out of a monitor. I refer to him as "the master of the tube alloys," unofficial code for his "research," a process which has appalling possibilities of destruction. To the straight world he's in public relations. We live in a carefully camouflaged ziggurat, located in a strategically situated community saturated by longing and guilt. The common room is only for thoughts — of sours, static and sprawl. My work has payed off, we're finally allowed entry into the blind alley, and a hail of bullets that can't look us in the eye. Gradually, the mirror reflects other hazes — one up, one more, one next to the Museum of Colored Glass and Light. By then we were under house arrest, and told to sacrifice the notion that we'd ever see the clouds below us.

Work

Beak dug both hands deep into the pockets of her pea coat. The fog machines prevented her from finding Doone. She had cabin fever big time, for those were the days of continous clock watching, back up against the wall (motherfucker). Shore leave was what made life worthwhile. Now she's an ambience coordinator. Mention her name and you'll get 10% off. All her clients are scented according to her specifications. The flowers are top heavy, but in their droop lies their funky allure. Beak and Doone scan the room and decide to eliminate all objects in the paprika family. It's a living. And what are you doing with your life that makes you think you're all that? "Personal expression"? Fling it against the wall; if it sticks it's part of the demographic. Beak and Doone complain that they can't get the smell off their hands. They just built a castle on the previously vacant lot across from Tower Video. They spend all of their spare time there, entertaining caged animals (boyfriends), looking forward to their retirement, when they can strip down to the bare essentials — scratching and sniffing.

Cup

I prefer the old world but that's just me. These cramped quarters have caused some of us to spontaneously combust. I managed to relocate to a kiosk with a Grover's Corner atmosphere. We always took pride in our appearance — splashing daily amongst the rocks — but once the sun had faded the earthen honeycomb we reverted to our post-homuncular existence. Whenever we looked at the world of interiors we saw red. The desire to be split open, turned inward, left a painful goose egg, and when we peered out we felt that familiar wave of compassion fatigue. We're our own best creations, cavorting in our lopsided tents of elbows, knees and nightgowns, half empty, half full, semi-automatic. The voice gradually faded away, the one telling us to stay put, at least for the time being.

One Thousand Five Hundred copies
of **TILT** printed August, 1996,
of which ten are numbered I-X
and signed by the poet.

Gillian McCain was born in New Brunswick, Canada in 1966. She attended the University of King's College in Halifax, Nova Scotia and New York University. She is the author of the chapbook Upside Down City, and the former editor of The Poetry Project Newsletter. From 1991-1994 she was the Program Coordinator of The Poetry Project at St. Mark's Church in Manhattan. She is the co-author (with Legs McNeil) of Please Kill Me: The Uncensored Oral History of Punk (Grove Press).